TABLE PRAYERS

Good Graces

Collected by Julie Jensen McDonald

Photography by Joan Liffring-Zug
Calligraphy by Esther Feske

A special thank-you for the people in the photographs—to Marcia Mays and Michael Phelan, and to the memory of three others: Peter Phelan, Dr. Henry Moershel and Marie Zuber.

Cover design by Mike Crilley
Book design by David Duer and Esther Feske
Edited by John Zug and Joan Liffring-Zug, Harry Oster, David Duer, Valerie Staats and Scott Elledge

Copyright © 1986 Penfield Press. All rights reserved.

Library of Congress Number 86-060322
ISBN 0-941016-31-5 cloth
ISBN 0-941016-32-3 paper
Printing: Julin Printing Company, Monticello, Iowa

Books by Mail (postpaid):

Good Graces (this book)
softbound $ 8.50
hardbound   18.50

A Diary of Personal Prayer
by Julie Jensen McDonald
softbound $ 10.50
hardbound   18.50

Scandinavian Proverbs
Collected by Julie Jensen McDonald
softbound $ 7.50
hardbound   18.50

Write for a complete list of our books:
Penfield Press
215 Brown Street
Iowa City, Iowa 52240-1358

JULIE JENSEN McDONALD is the author of three other Penfield Press titles: *Delectably Danish -Recipes and Reflections, Scandinavian Proverbs,* and *A Diary of Personal Prayer.* Her novels include *Amalie's Story, Petra,* and *The Sailing Out,* a trilogy about the lives of Danish women who came to America with their families, facing the hardships and victories of a new way of life. Other books by Julie Jensen McDonald include *Ruth Buxton Sayre,* a biography; *The Ballad of Bishop Hill,* the story of a Swedish colony in Illinois; and *Baby Black,* a children's book.

Julie is a graduate of the University of Iowa and holds an honorary Doctor of Letters degree from St. Ambrose College of Davenport, Iowa, where she teaches journalism.

Let me thank Thee
in prosperity
and
preserve my patience
in adversity.

—Saint Thomas Aquinas

TABLE OF CONTENTS

Front cover photo:
Religious books of The Community of True Inspiration, Amana, Iowa, on an antique pineapple-crocheted table cloth. (Courtesy Mrs. Adolph Schmieder.)
Back cover photo:
Antique butter churn from Sara Miller, member of the Old Order Amish, Kalona, Iowa.

EVERYDAY GRACE

Bless the bread winner,
the bread maker,
and all who are about
to break bread here.
You made us and sustain us, and
We praise Your name. Amen

—Julie Jensen McDonald

WHERE DO TABLE PRAYERS come from? When was the first expression of gratitude for food uttered - the first petition for blessing at table offered? Did the cavemen say thanks to someone or just dig in?

The answers to such questions are obscured by the mists of time, as investigation is restricted to the span of written history. I don't pretend to have inspected that whole span, but what I was able to find out by reading and questioning interested me greatly. I'm grateful to everyone who helped me in my search for good graces.

—*Julie Jensen McDonald*

Vesterheim, The Norwegian-American Museum

THE JUDEO-CHRISTIAN TRADITION has produced most of our table prayers, but pre-Christian Romans, Buddhists, Hindus, Muslims, and adherents of other world religions have voiced gratitude for nourishment, always necessary and frequently pleasurable.

For many, giving thanks for food is as natural as breathing and practiced with as little thought. Others never think of it because they never do it. Still others create fresh prayers for every meal in personal conversation with the Giver of table bounty.

Charles Lamb (1775-1834), English essayist and critic, must be credited with the most detailed consideration of the custom I have been able to find. In his *Essays of Elia* written in the 1820s, Lamb included "Grace Before Meat," a compendium of views both lyrical and humorous.

Lamb conjectured that the custom of saying grace at meals probably had its origin "in the early times of the world and the hunter-state of man, when dinners were precarious things, and a full meal was something more than a common blessing. When a belly full was a windfall and looked like a special providence."

He imagined the early hunters carrying home their "lucky booty of deer's or goat's flesh" with shouts and triumphal songs that were "perhaps, the germ of modern grace."

Lamb himself was "disposed to say grace upon twenty other occasions in the course of the day besides" his dinner—when setting out for a walk, during a moonlight ramble, enjoying a friendly meeting, or having solved a problem.

Calling graces "the sweet preluding strains to the banquets of angels and children," he approved most of benedictions at a poor man's table or before the simple repast of children: "It is here that grace becomes exceedingly graceful." He also appreciated the silent grace of Quakers.

Quite willing to scold, he wrote, "Would you have Christians sit down at table like hogs to their trough, without remembering the Giver?"

He also frowned on muttering "praises from a mouth that waters," and he took wry note of the etiquette of the custom, observing,

"In houses where the grace is as indispensable as the napkin, who has not seen that never-settled question arise as to who shall say it?"

Lamb reported that his old schoolfellow, C.V. LeGrice, often importuned to ask the blessing, would say, "Is there no clergyman here?," significantly adding, "Thank God!"

One needn't be ordained to ask a blessing at mealtime, and some of the most moving table prayers come from the "mouths of babes and sucklings." The family table is the place where many children learn to pray, and Mitch Finley, co-author with his wife Kathy of *Christian Families in the Real World,* says, "The most naturally prayerful time in the life of almost any family is the main meal of the day."

Let's go on, then, to the prayers themselves, building a grotto of the greatly varied petitions. The architecture will be eclectic, considering the contributions from many times and places, but the foundation is firm—the sincere devotion of good graces.

Other Faiths

The Upanishads, commentaries on the sacred writings of the ancient Hindus, may have exhorted in 600 B.C., "Let no man try to find out the tastes of food, let him know the knower of tastes," but even so, some of the Vedic hymns from the four collections of holy Hindu writings resemble food prayers:

> O wise Maruts, let us
> carry off the wealth of food
> you have bestowed on us.
>
> Grant to us, O immortal,
> the food of mortals.
> Be gracious to us
> and to our kith and kin.
>
> May this praise ask you
> for food for offspring,
> for ourselves. May we have
> invigorating autumn
> with quickening rain.

> O Rudras, come to us today
> with food,
> you much desired ones.

Buddhists find virtue in begging food with "appetite moderated," and the faithful believe that "giving away our food, we get more strength."

They are instructed to eat at proper times and to satisfy hunger "as the butterfly that sips the flower, not destroying its fragrance or texture."

The Koran of Islam comes closer to our understanding of food as a gift from the Creator. Muslims killing an animal for food must say "Bismillah " ("In the Name of God "), and if this utterance is neglected, they may not eat the meat lawfully. After their repast, the faithful say "Hemd'ullah " ("Thanks be to God ").

O God our Lord, cause a table
to descend unto us from heaven,
that the day of its descent may
become a festival day unto us;
and do Thou provide food for us,
for Thou art the best Provider.

—*The Koran*

O God, Thou providest food
to whom Thou wilt
without measure.

—*The Koran*

Ancient Rome

The agricultural religion of the ancient Romans glorified Ceres, goddess of the fertile earth, and Bacchus, god of the vine, but its adherents did not forget offerings to Jupiter, one of the more personal gods.

Fertile in fruits and in
herds, may the earth crown
Ceres with her spiky coronet.

Come to us, Bacchus, with the
cluster of sweet grapes hanging
from thy horns! And Ceres, bind
thy temples with ears of grain.

In offering thee this cake,
O Jupiter, I humbly pray that
thou, pleased with this offering,
will be propitious and merciful
to me and my children, my house
and my household.

Old Testament & Hebrew

The early Romans had to worry about praising the deity who could offer the most help without creating jealousy among the other gods. Offering thanks in the right quarter without fear of reprisal was a welcome advantage of monotheism.

> The Lord gives you in the
> evening flesh to eat
> and in the morning
> bread to the full.
> —*Exodus 16:8*

> You shall eat and be satisfied
> and bless the Lord your God.
> —*Deuteronomy 8:10*

> Bless the Lord, O my soul...
> Who satisfieth thy mouth with
> good things; so that thy youth
> is renewed like the eagle's.
> —*Psalms 103.5*

No one should taste anything
without first reciting a blessing
over it, as it is said, "The earth
is the Lord's, and its fullness."
Psalms 24:1. Whoever enjoys
the goods of this world
without reciting a blessing
has transgressed.

> —*Tosefta Berakhot*
> *Commentaries on the Talmud*

The following blessings come from *The
Daily Prayer Book:*

Praised are You, O Lord
our God, King of the Universe.
With goodness, with compassion,
and with kindness You graciously
nourish the whole world,
providing food for every
creature with everlasting mercy.
Your great goodness has never
failed us;

Your great glory assures us
nourishment. All life is Your
creation, and You are good to
all, providing every creature
with food and sustenance.
Praised are You, O Lord,
Who sustains all life.

The placemats used in an Illinois retirement home are printed with prayers of several faiths, including this traditional Hebrew blessing over bread:

Lift up your hands
toward the sanctuary
and bless the Lord.
Blessed are Thou,
O Lord our God,
King of the Universe,
Who bringest forth bread
from the earth.

Praised are you,
O Lord our God,
King of the Universe,
Who brings forth bread
from the earth.

—*The Daily Prayer Book*

New Testament

The story of the loaves and the fishes in two of the New Testament gospels (Mark and John) sets the chief precedent for giving thanks, and evidence that Christ's example was followed is found in the Pauline epistles.

> And He commanded the people
> to sit down on the ground: and
> He took the seven loaves and
> gave thanks, and brake, and
> gave to His disciples to
> set before them; and they did
> set them before the people.
> And they had a few small fishes:
> And He blessed and commanded
> to set them also before them. So
> they did eat and were filled.
>
> —*Mark 8:6-8*

He that eateth, eateth to
the Lord, for he giveth
God thanks.

—Romans 14:6

He (Paul) took bread and
gave thanks to God in the
presence of them all: and
when he had broken it, he
began to eat. Then were they
all of good cheer, and they
also took some meat.

—Acts 27:35-36

Paul counsels, "Giving thanks
always for all things unto God
and the Father in the Name of
our Lord Jesus Christ."

—Ephesians 5:20

Literary Graces

Not all great writers have been devout, but here is a sampling of the graces bequeathed to us by some who were.

From Saint Thomas Aquinas (1225-1274):

> Give us, O Lord, thankful
> hearts which never forget
> Your goodness to us.
> Give us, O Lord, grateful
> hearts, which do not waste
> time complaining.

From George Herbert (1593-1633):

> Our heavenly Father, Thou
> has provided us with all
> good things, so fill our
> hearts with Thy love and
> grace that we may use
> every gift to Thy glory.
> Amen.

It is very nice to think
The world is full of meat & drink,
with little children saying grace
In every Christian kind of place.

—Robert Louis Stevenson

From Robert Louis Stevenson (1850-1894):

Lord, behold our family here assembled.
We thank You for this place in which we dwell,
For the love that unites us,
For the peace accorded us this day.
For the hope with which we expect tomorrow;
For the health, the work, the food,
And the bright skies
that make our lives delightful.
Amen.

From Ralph Waldo Emerson (1803-1882):

> For health and food,
> for love and friends,
> for everything
> Thy goodness sends,
> Father in heaven,
> we thank Thee.

From Soren Kierkegaard (1813-1855):

> Lord our God! Every creature
> turns its eye to Thee and
> awaits its nourishment and
> subsistence from Thee. Thou
> openest Thy compassionate
> hand and Thou dost fill
> abundantly with blessing
> all who live.

> Oh, if at every meal something
> is wanting in case the blessing
> is lacking, what then might be
> this holy meal of grace without
> Thy blessing.

From Robert Burns (1759-1796):

Ye Powers Who gave us all that's good,
still bless auld Caledonia's brood
with great John Barleycorn's heart's bluide
in stupes and luggies. And on our board that
king o' food, a glorious haggis.

(The haggis is a heavenly hash of heart, liver,
and lungs cooked in a meticulously cleaned
sheep's stomach. "Bluide" is blood, "stupes" are
ladles, and "luggies" are bowls.)

> Fair fa' your honest, sonsie face,
> Great chieftain o' the pudding-race!
> Aboon them a' ye tak your place,
> Painch, tripe or thairm:
> Weel are ye wordy o' a grace
> as lang's my arm.
>   —*"Address to a Haggis"*

Who hasn't sent a prayer of thanks heaven-
ward for the first sweet corn of the season? Or
strawberries or asparagus? Each of us has our
favorite good thing, and gratitude for it surely
must be in order.

Robert Burns supposedly offered the Selkirk Grace while visiting the Earl of Selkirk at St. Mary's Isle, but some scholars now believe it originated in a Belfast newspaper around 1834. It is also known as the Covenanter's Grace:

Some have meat
        and cannot eat,
some cannot eat
        that want it;
But we have meat
        and we can eat,
so let the lord be thankit.

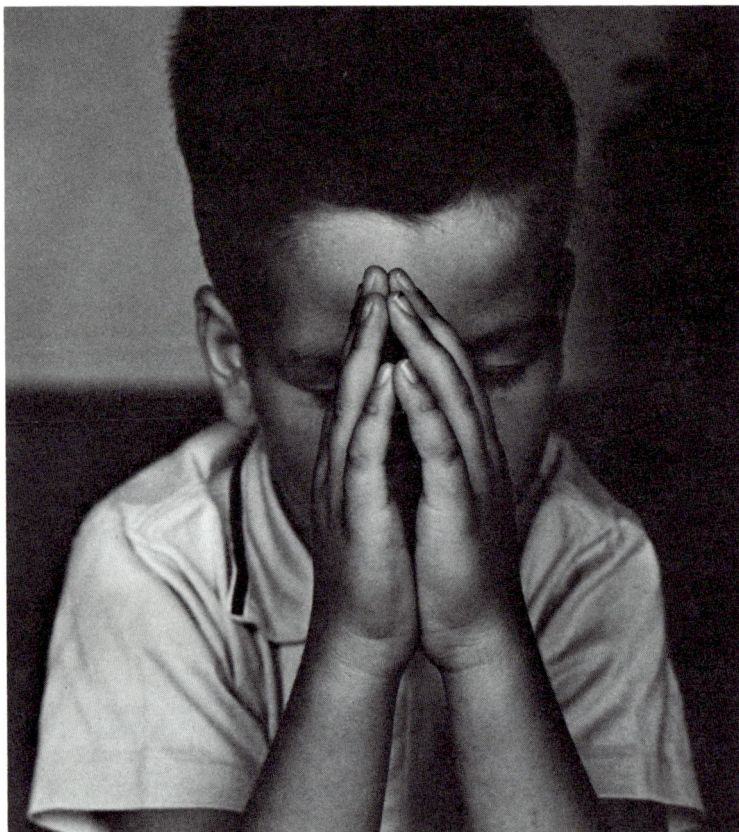

But I, when I undress me
Each night upon my knees
Will ask the Lord to bless me
With apple pie and cheese.

—*Eugene Field (1850-1895)*

Ancient & Anonymous Graces

Table prayers mellowed by centuries of use have special meaning, shared with the unseen cloud of witnesses who have prayed them before us. One theory of the identity of "Anonymous" authors is that the unnamed creators were female in a male-dominated age. This may be so in the shaping of prayers, and if not, women surely were the conservators of well-loved graces, passing them from age to age.

> Let us in peace
> eat the food
> God has provided
> for us.
> Praise be to God
> for all His gifts.
> Amen.
>
> —*Ancient Armenian grace*

Sanctify this milk that has been
pressed into cheese, and press us
together in charity. Grant that
this fruit of the olive tree may
never lose its savor; for the
olive is a symbol of that
abundance which, at Your
bidding, flowed from the tree
and is there for those who
trust You. Amen.

—Second century Greek blessing

I thank Thee for fresh leeks,
for speckled salmon, for plump
hens and bees.
I thank Thee for my fill of
clothing and food
And for the right to raise
this prayer. Amen.

—Adapted from tenth century
Celtic meditation

This ancient prayer which turns up everywhere, including the wall of England's Chester Cathedral, has been attributed to Thomas H.B. Webb:

Give me a good digestion, Lord,
and also something to digest;
Give me a healthy body, Lord,
and sense to keep it at its best;
Give me a healthy mind, good Lord,
to keep the good and pure in sight,
Which, seeing sin, is not appalled,
But finds a way to set it right.

Give me a mind that is not bound,
that does not whimper, whine, or sigh.
Don't let me worry overmuch
about the fussy thing called I.
Give me a sense of humor, Lord;
Give me the grace to see a joke,
To get some happiness from life
and pass it on to other folk.

The fourteenth - century English mystic, Julian of Norwich, included the following meditation in her *Revelations of Divine Love* and it seems appropriate for this collection:

> I saw in my imagination heaven,
> and our Lord as the head of His
> own house, who had invited all
> His dear servants and friends to
> a great feast. The Lord, I saw,
> occupied no one place in
> particular in His house, but
> presided regally over it all,
> suffusing it with joy and
> cheer. . .

> God bless this food,
> And bless us all,
> And keep us safe,
> Whate'er befall,
> For Jesus' sake. Amen.
> *—Anonymous*

> May the Blessed One
> bless us. Amen.
> *—Anonymous*

God bless the master of this house,
   God bless the mistress too,
      and all the little children
         that 'round the table go.

—*Anonymous*

Graces From Many Lands

Prayers translated from other languages may lose some of their flavor, but the essence of thankfulness survives, along with the cultural tone of national character.

> May the blessing of five
> loaves and two fishes
> which God divided amongst
> Five thousand men be ours,
> And may the King Who made
> division put luck in our
> food and in our portion.
> Amen.
>
> *—Irish meal prayer*

> O Christ our God, bless the
> food and drink of thy servants,
> For Thou art Holy always, now
> and ever and unto ages of ages.
> Amen.
>
> *—Greek Orthodox grace*

Dear God, bless those who
bear the hardship of famine
and those who share their
plenty with others.
Wrap Thy love around those
who come to us in trust
and take care of those who
wander far from us in anger.
Amen.

—Early Hawaiian food prayer

O Lord of the harvest, Giver
of our daily bread, we rejoice
in all Thy fatherly goodness and
pray that Thy loving kindness
may so prevail in the hearts of
Thy children everywhere that
the earth may be filled with
gladness and peace, through
Jesus Christ our Lord. Amen.

—Scottish grace

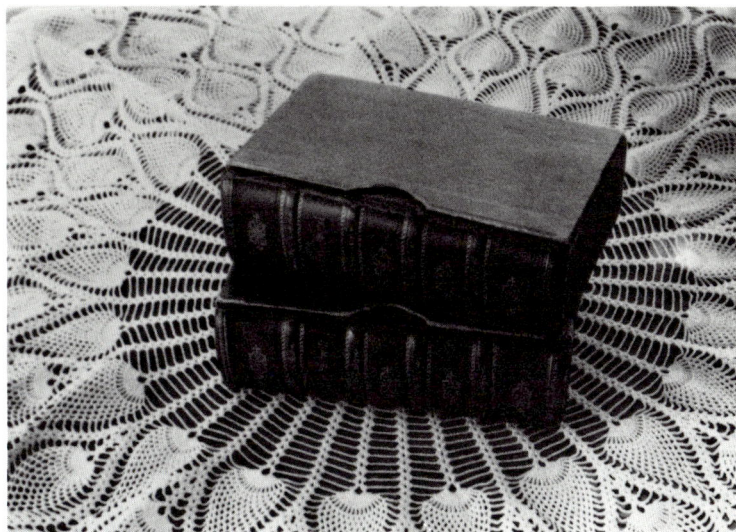

For all your goodness
and this meal,
receive, kind Lord,
our thanks and praise.
Amen

—*Swedish table prayer*

Fill us with thankfulness for all
Thy temporal gifts; And since it
is not by bread alone that man
lives, Grant us evermore to
give thanks to Thee for Him
Who is the true bread that
came down from heaven, Jesus
Christ our Lord. Amen.

—Church of Scotland

Sportsmen probably have shaped their special prayers as long as humankind has relished the chase.

Dear God, We thank Thee
for this good, honest
wholesome, hungry breakfast
and ask Thy help in catching
lunch and dinner. Amen.

—Fisherman's prayer
after Isaak Walton

Bless us, dear Lord, and the food
received from Thy holy bounty.
In the Name of Christ, Amen.

—Boundary Waters, Minnesota
Hunter's grace

O God, make us able
for what's on the table.
amen

—*An Irish prayer*

Religious books of the Old Order Amish, Kalona, Iowa. Courtesy Sara Miller.

Churchly Graces

Although the shaping of mealtime praise and petition is frequently the work of lay persons, theological professionals have contributed heavily to the annals of table prayers.

These graces are from *A Year With The Bible* by Hugh T. Kerr of the Princeton Theological Seminary faculty (Westminster Press, Philadelphia, Pa., 1984):

> Sustain our bodies with this food,
> our hearts with true friendship,
> and our souls in Christian love.
> Amen.
>
> For all good gifts we offer
> thanks: for food and shelter, for
> health and strength, for friends
> and family, for memories of the
> past and hopes for the future,
> for the inspiration of the
> Scriptures and the fellowship of
> the church, and especially for

Jesus Christ, who brought life
and immortality to light. Glory
hallelujah! Amen.

May we be grateful for all
mercies and ask for God's
blessing. Amen.

Almighty God, in providing for
us, nourish our souls with the
bread of life in Christ. Amen.

Make us thankful to God and
mindful of others as we receive
all our blessings. Amen.

O Almighty Father, from Whom
cometh every good and perfect
gift, we humbly thank Thee for
all Thy mercies. We thank Thee
for creation, preservation, and
redemption; for all Thy gifts of
nature and of grace; for health
and strength, for homes and
kindred, for true friends and
wise teachers; for all the

blessings of this life and for
our hope of a better life to
come. Amen.

—*Church of Scotland*

Sister Ritamary Bradley, S.F.C.C. (Sisters
for Christian Community) contributes the following graces which she usually personalizes
with names:

Jesus, one with the Trinity,
thank You for gathering us
together to break bread in Your
name. Grant us sustenance in
body, mind, and spirit, through
the bread we eat and through
the friendship that this meal
shows forth and sustains.
Amen.

Heavenly Parent, thank
You for the bread that comes to
us from Your hands. In Your
name we remember those who
have been close to us and have
left this life. In Your name we

pray for those who suffer and
are in want. May this time of
joyful sharing bear abundant
fruit in our lives. Through
Jesus Christ, who became one of us.
Response: God bless the cook!

(Sister Ritamary says the response is anonymous
and traditional.)

Communal prayers before meals at the
Carmelite Monastery in Eldridge, Iowa are
adapted from the *Ritual for Carmelite Nuns:*

COMMUNAL PRAYER BEFORE MEALS

Leader: Praise the Lord.
All: May the Lord be praised.
Leader: The eyes of all
All: Hope in You, O Lord, for
You give them food in due
season. You open Your hand
and fill all creatures with Your
blessing. Glory be to the Father, and

to the Son, and to the Holy
Spirit, as it was in the begin-
ning, is now, and ever shall
be—world without end. Amen.
Leader: Lord, have mercy on us.
All: Christ, have mercy on us.
Leader: Let us all recite the
Lord's Prayer together.
All: Our Father. . . *(continue*
with the Lord's Prayer).
Leader: Bless us, O Lord, and
these Your gifts, which we are
about to receive from Your
bounty through Christ our
Lord.
All: Amen.
Leader: May the King of
Everlasting Glory give us a
place at His heavenly table.

SUPPER PRAYER

Leader: Praise the Lord.
All: Let us praise the Lord.

Leader: The poor will eat
All: And receive their fill. Those
who seek the Lord will praise
Him and will live forever. Glory
be to the Father, and to the Son,
and to the Holy Spirit, as it was
in the beginning, is now, and
ever shall be - world without
end. Amen.
Leader: Let us all recite the
Lord's Prayer together.
All: Our Father. . . *(Lord's
Prayer follows).*
Leader: Bless us, O Lord, and
these Your gifts which we are
about to receive from Your
bounty through Christ our
Lord.
All: Amen.
Leader: May the King of
Everlasting Glory bring us to
His heavenly banquet.
All: Amen.

A GRACE AFTER MEALS

All may say the whole prayer or one side of the table may start and the other side may finish it.

Walk through life with the
Lord giving thanks; enter His
courts with words of praise.
Give thanks to Him and bless
His name.

Yes, God is good, His love is
everlasting. His faithfulness
endures from age to age.

On Sundays, the Carmelites sing a traditional grace to music written by Sister Mary Anne, O.C.D., both before and after meals. It is on the following page.

Sung Grace
before & after meals

Sister Mary Anne, O.C.D.
Carmelite Monastery
Eldridge, Iowa

Bless us, O Lord, and these Your gifts,
We give You thanks, al-might-y God for

which we are a-bout   to re-ceive from Your boun-
all the ben-e-fits we have re-ceived from Your boun-

ty through Je-sus Christ our Lord. A-   men.
ty through Je-sus Christ our Lord. A-   men.

O God of Bethel, by whose hand
Thy people still are fed,
Who through this weary
pilgrimage has all our fathers
led; our vows, our prayers, we
now present before Thy throne
of grace; God of our fathers, be
the God of their succeeding race.

—*Philip Doddridge (1702-1751)*

The God of love my Shepherd is,
and He that doth me feed,
While He is mine, and I am His,
What can I want or need?
Amen.

—*George Herbert (1593-1633)*

The following two graces can be sung to
the tune of "Old Hundred," a familiar musical
setting for the Psalms when the words and
music of hymns were composed separately.

Lord Jesus, be our holy guest,
Our morning joy, our evening rest,
And with our daily bread impart
Your love and peace to every heart.

Be present at our table, Lord,
Be here and everywhere adored;
These mercies bless and grant that we
May strengthened for Thy service be.

The three following graces are from *The Presbyterian Worshipbook* (Westminster Press, Philadelphia, Pa., 1975):

Father (or Mother): Praise the Lord!
Family: The Lord's Name be praised!
Parent: Let us thank God,
Family: For He is good!
All: Amen.

God, we thank You for home,
family and friends. May Your
love be with us as we break
bread in Jesus' name. Amen.

Thank You, God, for food
and all Your gifts,
Through Jesus Christ our Lord.
Amen.

Bless us, O Lord, and these,
Your gifts, which we are
about to receive through
Christ our Lord. Amen.
                    —*Catholic table prayer*

Decades ago, saying grace in college dining
rooms was not unheard of, and here's one
remembered by some graduates of a college in
Ohio:

We thank Thee, O Lord, for Thy
mercies, which are new every
morning and fresh every evening.
Help us in return to give Thee
the supreme love of our hearts
and the full service of our
lives for His name's sake.
Amen.

BLESS ⬦ LORD

this food to our use
and us to thy service,
and keep us mindful
of the needs of others,
for Christ's sake:

AMEN

—*My Book of Prayers*

Children's Graces

The folding of small hands and the sincerity of young voices gives special poignance to the table prayers of children. Many of us learned our best-loved graces when we were very young, and we still recite them silently as a tiny voice offers them aloud.

God is great, God is good;
Let us thank Him for our food.
By His hand we all are fed.
Give us, Lord, our daily bread.
—The most familiar table grace

Fern Parker of Moline, Illinois remembers these childhood prayers fondly:

Thank You, God
for milk and bread
and other good things
we are fed.

Thank You, God
for those who help
to grow and cook my food.

Come, Lord Jesus, be our guest
and let Thy gifts to us be blessed.

Thank You, kind Father, for
giving us food to make our
bodies grow stronger. Dear God,
teach us to share with others
what we ourselves have. Amen.

—A child's prayer from China

Father God, please give to us
a fat dumpling on the table,
a fat patty in the pan,
today and evermore. Amen.

—A child's prayer
from Salzburg, Austria

(From *Children's Prayers from Other Lands*, selected
by Dorothy Gladys Spicer, Association Press,
New York, 1955.)

The comfort of custom makes the oft-heard graces so endearing. As new familes are formed, customs are combined, and we enrich the fabric of our experience. Fortunately, good graces never wear out. Georgia Heald of Iowa City, Iowa says that her family further personalized the custom of holding hands during grace by adding the "squeeze". The person offering the prayer would start the loving pressure around the table, and when it returned to him or her, the "Amen" would be said and the meal would begin.

Family prayers passed from generation to generation include the following:

Come, Lord Jesus, be our guest,
Our morning joy, our evening rest;
with this daily bread impart
the truest joy to every heart.

—Pamela Long Clark
Davenport, Iowa

We thank Thee, Heavenly Father,
for this food and for our
blessings this day; we ask
of Thee, forgive us our sins,
in Jesus' name. Amen.

—Grace from West Virginia Methodists

These blessings are from *My Book of Prayers*
(published by the Augustana Book Concern,
Rock Island, Illinois):

We thank Thee for our daily bread,
Let also, Lord, our souls be fed.
Oh, Bread of Life, from day to day,
sustain us on our homeward way.
Amen.

For food and all Thy gifts of love,
we give Thee thanks and praise;
Look down, O Father, from above,
and bless us all our days.
Amen.

Who can fail to be moved by the prayers of one's grandchildren? Here are two from the author's:

> Dear God, take care of
> that little boy in Ecuador.
> Give him food and money. Amen.
>
> *—Jill Pearson, age 2*

> Dear Lord, Thank You for
> this food. Help me to be
> a good girl. Be with us
> when we go to church. Amen.
>
> *—Erika Pearson, age 4*

Custom-Made Graces
from the author's family

A European priest once said that standard prayers were best for mealtime use—not too long. He recommended a lifting of the eyes and a warm *Thank You* rather than a lengthy before- or after-dinner speech.

Because our lives change from day to day, our family often feels a need to get specific in table prayers. Even when we don't have special necessities, we tend to make our prayers "from scratch".

Father, thank you for this day
and what we were able to accomplish.
Thank You for this food
and for all Your provisions.
Be with us as we spend
this evening together.

—*The Reverend Scott Pearson*
Ely Baptist Church, Minnesota
(Author's son-in-law)

Dear Lord, bless everyone
around this table and those
who are far away. Bless this
food to our bodies' use. Amen.

—Jack McDonald
(Author's husband)

The rest are the author's, fashioned according to the dictates of the heart on any given day.

THANKSGIVING DAY

Father, we thank You for the
plenteous meal You have
enabled us to prepare. We
pray for our brothers and
sisters everywhere that they
may not go hungry on this day.
Amen.

BUSY DAY GRACE

We come to the table in Jesus' name,
praising God for whatever we find there.
Amen.

POTLUCK PRAYER

God, we thank Thee for the skill
of the hands that prepared this food
and for the pleasure and nourishment
this meal provides. Amen.

GRACE AFTER THE 6 P.M. NEWS

Father, as we partake of Thy
good provision, we pray for the
hungry who have no food and for those
who have no heart to eat.
Help us to share what we have and
take no blessing for granted. Amen.

GRACE ON A TIRING DAY

Father, bless all who are gathered
at this table and those we love
who are not with us here.
May the breaking of bread give us
the strength and cheer to spread
Thy love. Amen.

AMEN AND AMEN